Sharks
and Rays

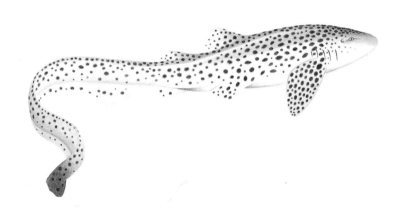

Text: Sharon Dalgleish

Consultant: Craig Sowden, Curator, Sydney Aquarium

This edition first published 2003 by

MASON CREST PUBLISHERS INC.

370 Reed Road

Broomall, PA 19008

© Weldon Owen Inc.

Conceived and produced by

Weldon Owen Pty Limited

Library of Congress Cataloging-in-Publication Data
on file at the Library of Congress

ISBN: 1-59084-170-0

Printed in Singapore.

1 2 3 4 5 6 7 8 9 06 05 04 03

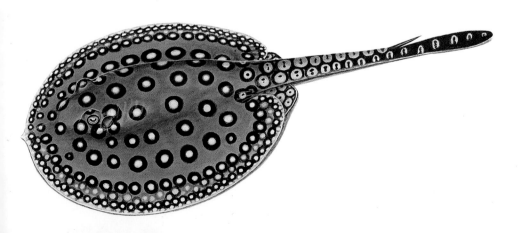

CONTENTS

WHAT ARE SHARKS?

Sharks belong to the same group of fish as rays. Most fish have a skeleton made of bone. Sharks and rays don't have bones. They have a skeleton made of cartilage. Feel your ear. It's made of cartilage, too. Many people are afraid of sharks, even though most sharks don't attack people.

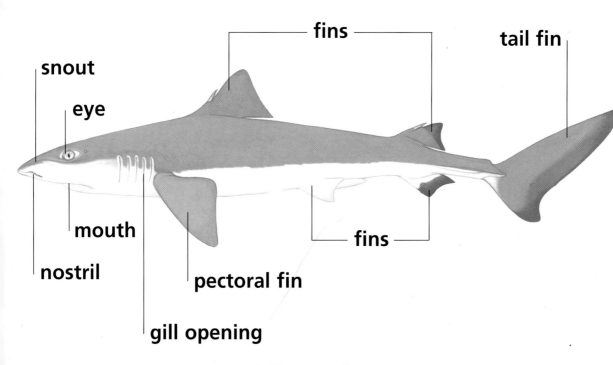

snout

eye

fins

tail fin

mouth

fins

nostril

pectoral fin

gill opening

A TYPICAL SHARK

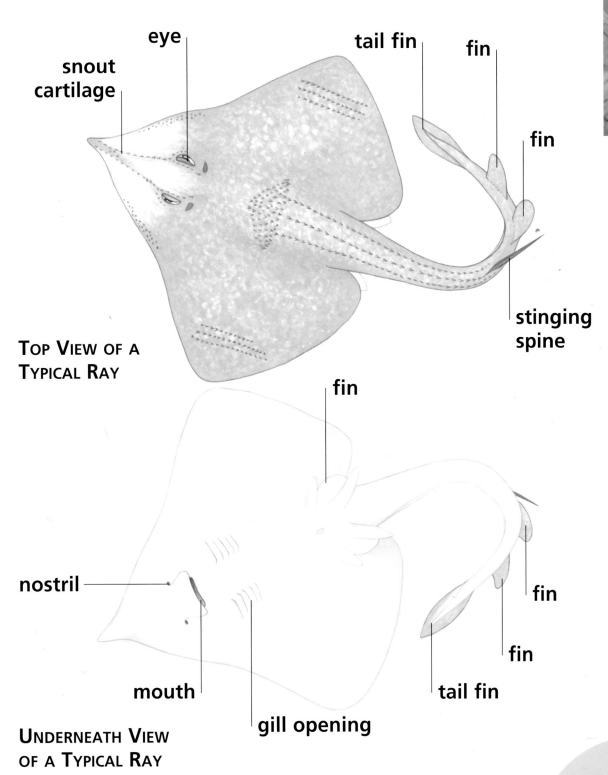

eye

snout
cartilage

tail fin

fin

fin

stinging
spine

**TOP VIEW OF A
TYPICAL RAY**

fin

nostril

fin

fin

mouth

tail fin

gill opening

**UNDERNEATH VIEW
OF A TYPICAL RAY**

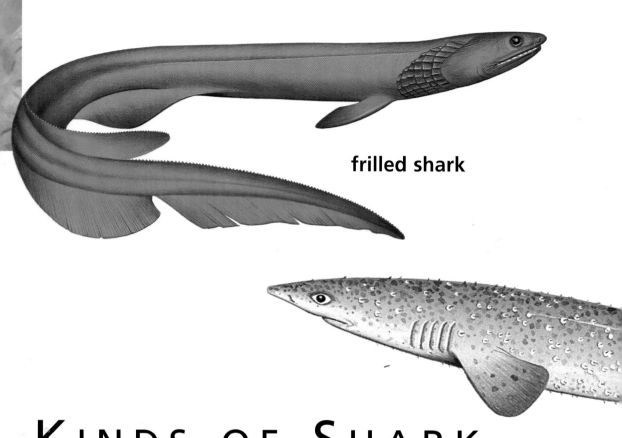

frilled shark

KINDS OF SHARK

There are more than 350 kinds of shark. Look at the sharks on the next four pages. They are all different. Frilled sharks have a head that looks like a snake. Angel sharks look like they have been flattened. Bramble sharks have a long snout. Saw sharks look like they have a saw for a snout.

angel shark

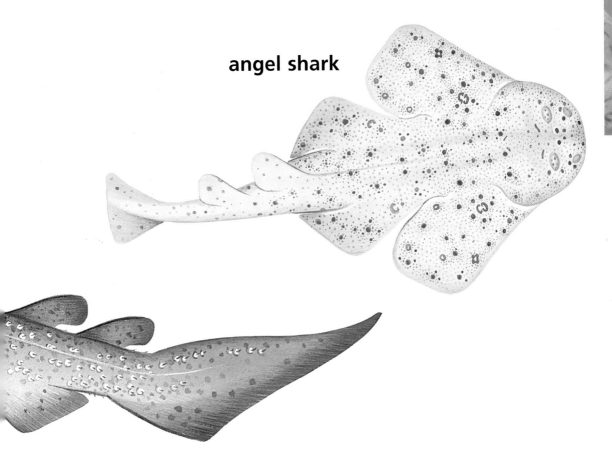

bramble shark

saw shark

7

The skin of zebra sharks changes
from stripes to spots as they get older. Horn
sharks have a snout like a pig. Oceanic whitetip
sharks have long pectoral fins that look like paddles.
The top part of the thresher shark's tail fin is huge.
It's as long as the rest of its body!

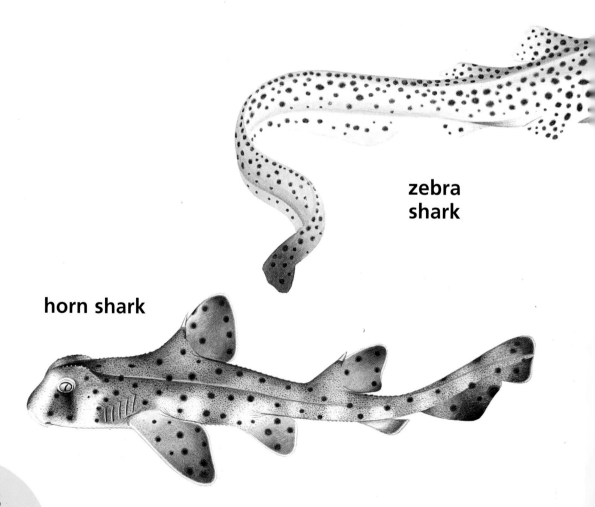

zebra
shark

horn shark

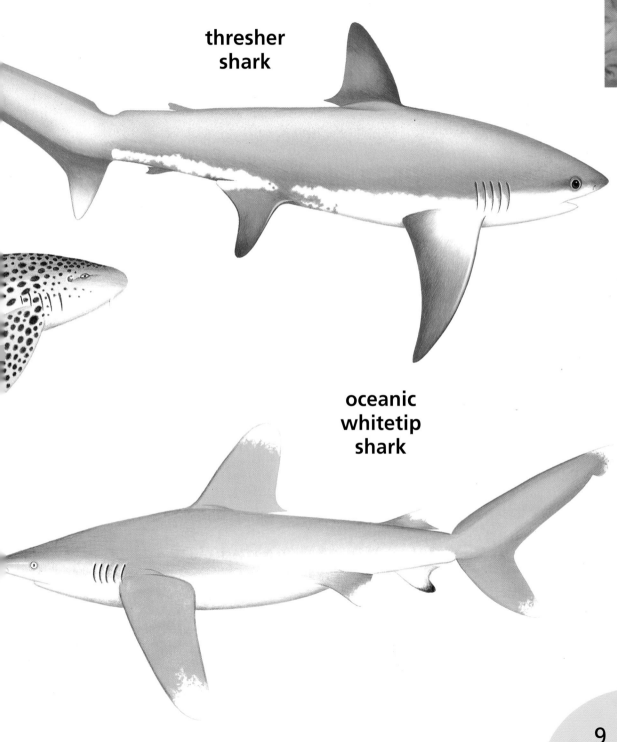

thresher
shark

oceanic
whitetip
shark

manta ray

sawfish

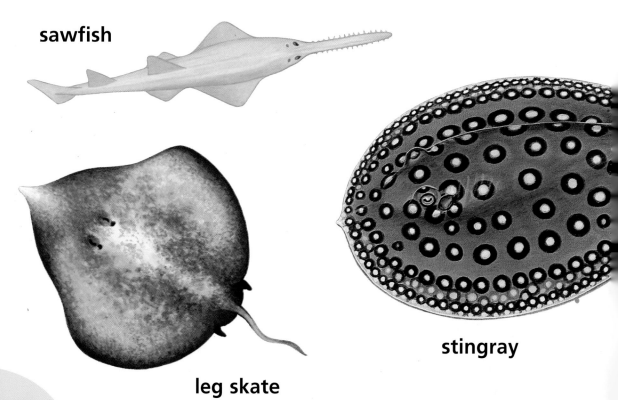

leg skate

stingray

KINDS OF RAY

There are about 600 kinds of ray that we know of, and more species are still being discovered. The huge manta ray is the biggest. It can be more than 20 feet (6.7 meters) wide. The short-nosed electric ray is the smallest. It's only about 4 inches (10 centimeters) wide.

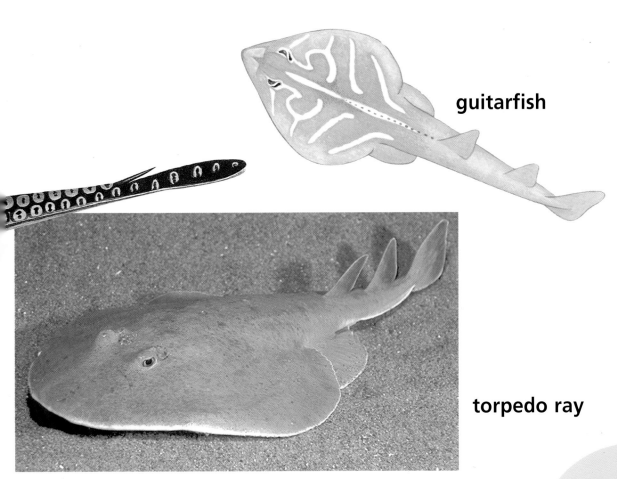

guitarfish

torpedo ray

SHARK SIZES

Sharks come in all sizes, but most are smaller than people. The largest shark is the whale shark. It can grow to 45 feet (14 meters) but is harmless, only filter-feeding on plankton and small fish. One of the smallest sharks is the spined pygmy shark. It grows to just 6 inches (15 centimeters).

bonnethead

white shark

How Big?
These sharks have been drawn to scale. You can see how big they are by comparing them with the human diver.

tasseled wobbegong

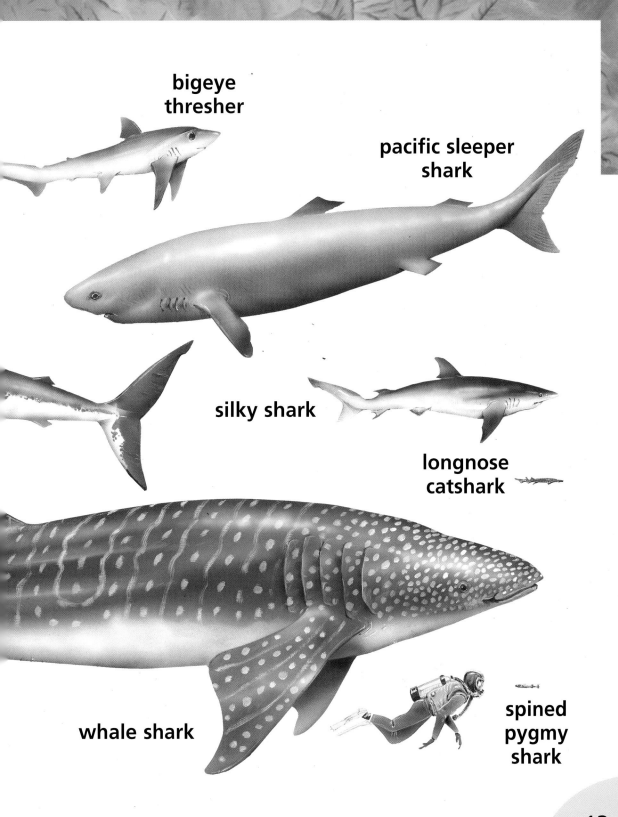

bigeye
thresher

pacific sleeper
shark

silky shark

longnose
catshark

whale shark

spined
pygmy
shark

oceanic whitetip shark

blue shark

goblin shark

megamouth

crocodile shark

spiny dogfish

lanternshark

pygmy shark

cookiecutter shark

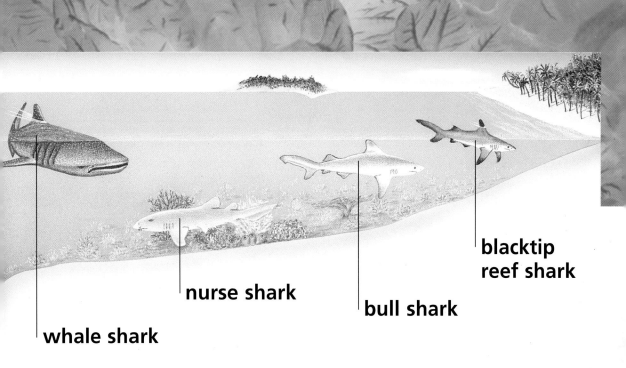

blacktip
reef shark

nurse shark

bull shark

whale shark

WHERE SHARKS LIVE

Different sharks live in different parts of the ocean.
They live where they can find the food they like to
eat. Some live near the coast, others live on reefs
and some live in the open ocean. Some sharks live
in the top level of the ocean where the water is
warmer. Some live in the middle level where the
water is colder. A few live at the dark bottom
of the deep sea.

SHARK SHAPES

To get a clue to a shark's way of life, look at the shape of its body. The blue shark is a graceful swimmer. Water flows smoothly over its body. The mako shark is one of the fastest swimmers. It's shaped like a torpedo. The angel shark has a flat body. It likes to lie buried in the sand on the ocean floor.

blue shark

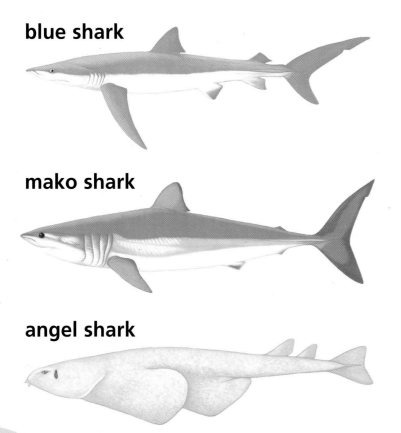

mako shark

angel shark

Tail Shapes
Sharks use their tail to move forward. In fast sharks, the two parts of the tail are almost the same size.

nurse shark tail

DID YOU KNOW?

The silky shark is a very fast swimmer but it doesn't turn gracefully. It changes direction with a sudden darting movement.

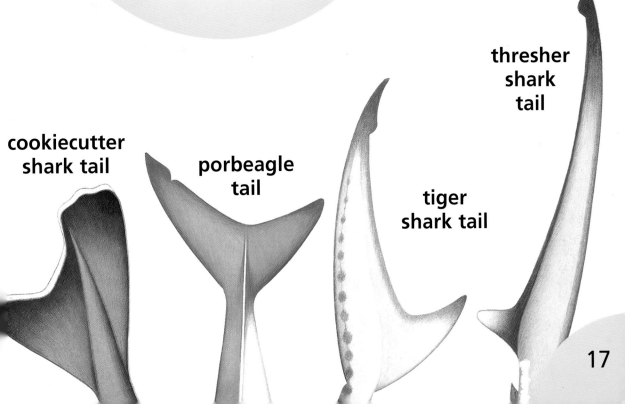

cookiecutter
shark tail

porbeagle
tail

tiger
shark tail

thresher
shark
tail

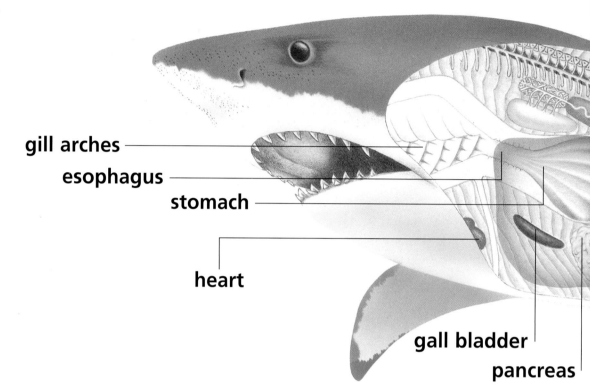

gill arches

esophagus

stomach

heart

gall bladder

pancreas

INSIDE A SHARK

Packed inside a shark's sleek body are all the organs it needs to breathe, eat, and even float. The shark's liver is huge and rich in oil. Oil is lighter than water and floats, which helps to stop the heavy shark from sinking. It's like having built-in water wings! A shark's backbone goes right into the top part of the tail. This makes the tail very powerful.

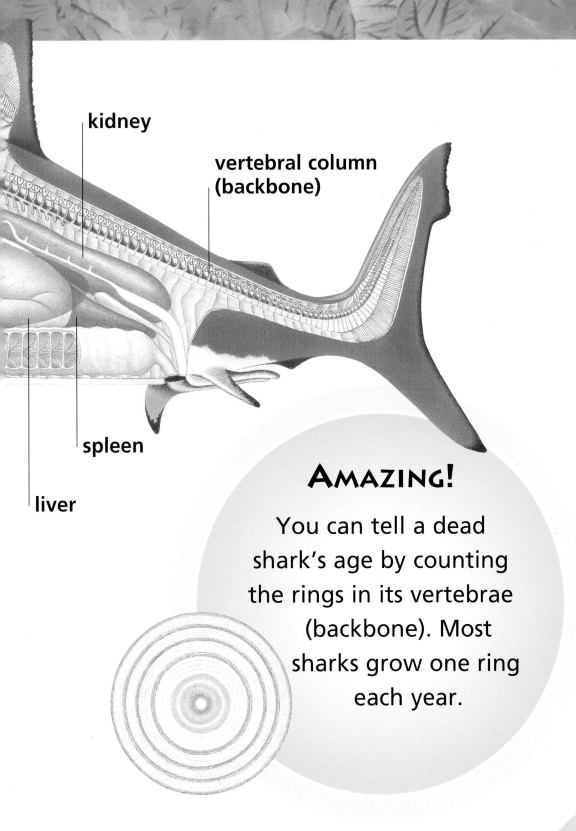

kidney

vertebral column
(backbone)

spleen

liver

AMAZING!

You can tell a dead shark's age by counting the rings in its vertebrae (backbone). Most sharks grow one ring each year.

SENSES

Just like you, sharks can see, hear, smell, taste, and touch. They also have a sense that lets them feel vibrations in the water. Tubes, called the lateral line system, run down each side of a shark's body. Smaller tubes connect the main tubes to the skin. Tiny cells like hairs inside the small tubes pick up any movement.

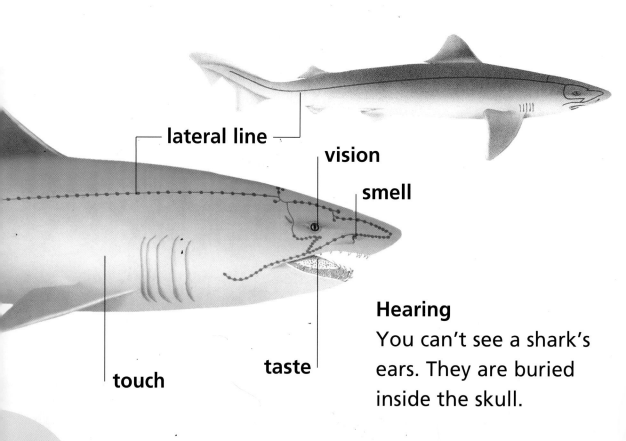

lateral line

vision

smell

touch

taste

Hearing
You can't see a shark's ears. They are buried inside the skull.

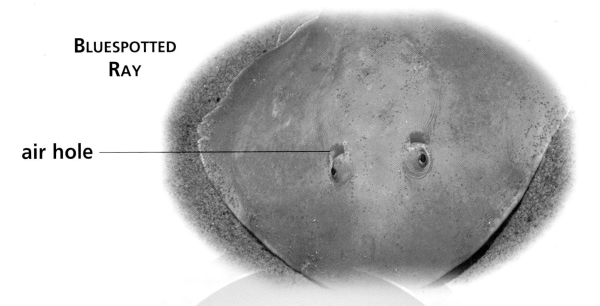

BLUESPOTTED RAY

air hole

DID YOU KNOW?

Sharks and rays that lie flat on the sea bed have eyes on top of their head. A bluespotted ray has eyes on short stalks.

ANGEL SHARK

BREATHING

Sharks and rays breathe by taking oxygen out of the water. In fast-swimming sharks, water rushes into the mouth as the shark swims. This water passes over the gills and then out the gill openings. Great white sharks have to keep swimming or they will stop breathing. Other sharks have a gill pump to keep the water flowing in.

How Gills Work
As water passes over the gills, oxygen is taken out.

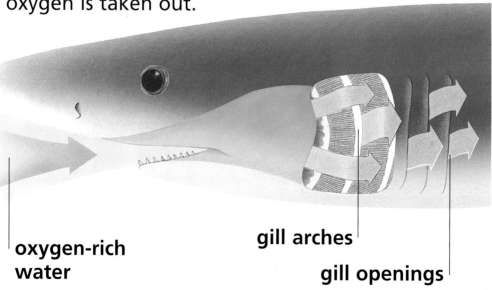

oxygen-rich
water

gill arches

gill openings

BREATHING ON THE BOTTOM

Rays can still breathe when they lie buried in the sand. They take water in through a hole behind each eye on top of the head. The water is then pumped out the gill openings underneath.

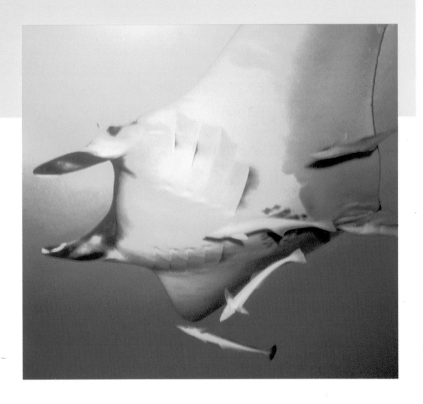

TAKE A BITE

Shark teeth come in many shapes and sizes. It depends on the food a shark eats. Some sharks don't eat with their teeth. They have rows of bristles to filter food out of the water. Sharks don't have to worry about their teeth getting blunt or broken. They just keep growing new teeth whenever they need them.

Power Jaws
The great white shark lifts its snout and opens wide. The upper jaw comes right out of the mouth and … snap! One bite is all it takes to kill.

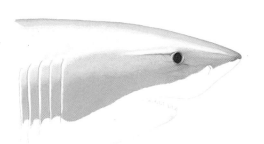

Stage one   **Stage two**

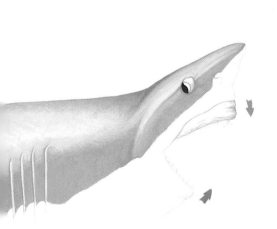

goblin shark teeth

DID YOU KNOW?

Shark scales are made of the same material as shark teeth. That's why shark skin feels like sandpaper. It's like being covered in thousands of tiny teeth!

great white shark teeth

Stage three

Stage four

ATTACK!

Some sharks have bitten and killed people. A shark might attack if it thinks it is in danger. Sometimes a shark might mistake a person for food, particularly if the person is splashing around. It's not a good idea to swim where there are turtles or seals, which are the normal food of large sharks.

Mistaken Identity
This surfer had a lucky escape after a hungry shark took a bite out of his surfboard. The shark probably thought the surfer was a turtle or a seal.

BEACH NETS

At some beaches, nets are stretched through shallow waters to keep swimmers safe from sharks. Some people don't like the nets because they also trap and kill harmless sharks, rays, turtles, and dolphins. Beach nets are very expensive. They need to be checked nearly every day to remove dead animals and they have to be repaired after storms.

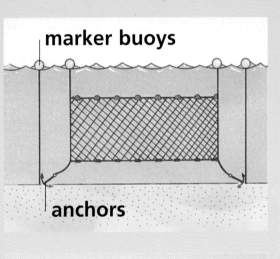

marker buoys

anchors

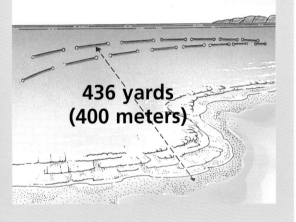

436 yards
(400 meters)

Sharks use sign language. A shark will often signal before it attacks. Some sharks swim straight at a threat and then turn away at the last moment, flicking their tail to make a loud cracking sound. Other sharks swim in loops, getting closer and closer. It's a bluff to avoid a fight!

DID YOU KNOW?

Stingrays have poisonous spines in their tails. The sting from some rays is painful. The sting from other rays can kill a person.

Normal Swimming

This gray reef shark (right) is swimming normally. Its back has a graceful curve. Its side fins are straight out from its body.

side view

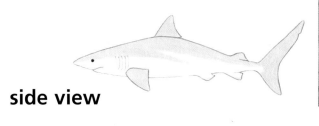

front view

top view

side view

front view

Ready to Attack

This gray reef shark (left) is swimming with an arched back. Its side fins are pointed downward. Its head and tail wag from side to side. If the threat does not back away, this shark may attack.

top view

29

GLOSSARY

buoy A float with an anchor used to mark a special place in the water.

cartilage Solid, elastic material inside an animal. Cartilage helps to support the shape of some fish, like bones do in humans.

filter-feeding The feeding method of some sharks, by swimming with the mouth open to catch food in the rows of bristles inside.

reef A narrow ridge of rock or coral in the sea.

skeleton The framework, made of bone or cartilage, inside the body of an animal.

species A group of animals or plants that share the same main features. Members of the same species can mate and breed.

INDEX

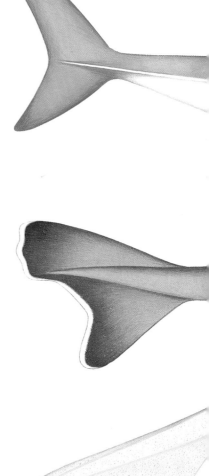

PICTURE AND ILLUSTRATION CREDITS

BOOKS IN THIS SERIES